A WELSH WOMAN'S VIEW

A WELSH WOMAN'S VIEW

by

BRENDA JONES

Edited by

Mike Willmott

FRONT COVER DESIGN

Gerald Newton

www.shrewsburybooks.com

136 FRANKWELL QUAY, SHREWSBURY SY3 8JX
Tel. 01743-366933 Mob. 07796-375798
mikewillmott@unicombox.co.uk
www.shrewsburybooks.com

Printed by Coton Print, 19 Whitehall Street, Shrewsbury

DEDICATION

for my mother, and all my family,
and all who have supported me in this venture

A proportion of the profits from this project will be donated

to the ALZHEIMER'S SOCIETY,

towards their Research Project.

CONTENTS

Introduction

I was born in Oswestry, to Welsh-speaking parents. I lived in Llanfyllin until I was six years old. We moved to Efailrhyd, Llanrhaeadr-ym-Mochnant, and I was educated at Cefnhirfach Primary School, Llanfyllin High School, and Wrexham Technical College. I worked as a secretary until my marriage to a Welsh dairy farmer, and still live on that same farm in Cefn Canol, near Llansilin. I have two grown-up children, and my family and the countryside are my main sources of inspiration. I have been writing poetry for the past twenty years.

The main spur to publish this book was encouragement by friends and family. I was also asked by a number of local organizations e.g. Rhydycroesau Ladies' Guild, Llansilin Over 60s Club and Llanfyllin Mothers' Union, to recite some of my poems. I was forever being asked, "Why don't you publish a book?" Also, my mother died two and a half years ago, after suffering from Alzheimer's for some years. I have written four poems, one about my mother having Alzheimer's, one about the general effects of the disease (with some humour), one about mum's time in a nursing home and another about euthanasia. I have also tried to look at the lighter side of the disease. My husband has often said, had we not laughed at some of the things mum did, we would have cried. I found that in writing these poems, they had a cathartic effect on me.

I found a telephone number on the back of a poem book I'd bought some years before. The lady I spoke to gave me Mike Willmott's telephone number. I spoke to Mike at some length, and decided he was the person I wanted to edit my book. After some initial sparring, we worked together quite harmoniously. He was able to make my poems look quite presentable. Some of his favourite words are "doggerel," "tautology" and "collaboration." My use of the English language has improved considerably since meeting Mike. It has been a pleasure working with him. Mike then introduced me to Gerald Newton, the illustrator responsible for the colourful cover of the book. The illustrations hint at some of my poems.

ROOTS

WALES

I'm proud of my homeland,
the green hills of Wales;
the wonderful scenery,
and all the folk tales.

The peace and the quiet,
as I walk the hills;
my sheepdog beside me,
enjoying the views.

The sound of the choirs
echo in my mind:
well known for our singing,
and love of mankind.

The lilt of our language –
it makes me so proud
I'm able to speak it.
I'll shout it out loud:

our success with rugby,
and games that we play.
So, close to my heart,
Wales, for ever, will stay.

BRYN TIRION
memories of Dad, and Bryn Tirion – first home

First memories that I recall
stem from the time when I was small,
walking to meet you off the train —
you bringing me a toy or game.

Topsi singed himself one morning
by the fire he was warming.
Into my basket he would go
sliding on a slippery floor.

Topsi jumping up to scare me;
Mr. Pastry on the telly;

1

Perry Mason, and What's my Line?
If only I could turn back time.

Had a tricycle for Christmas —
riding it, a tricky business.
A girl, she fell whilst on her horse:
you going there to help of course.

Seeing pigs on Sunday morning:
Fling, she died without a warning.
I may not speak of these, and yet —
you can be sure, I won't forget.

MY CHILDHOOD CHRISTMAS

On Christmas Eve, when I was young
a-shopping we would go,
to buy last minute presents,
and see the goods on show.

When finally I'd get to bed,
how long the night would seem:
to say I was excited
was mild in the extreme.

I'd always try and stay awake,
to catch a glimpse of Him.
But every time I'd fall asleep,
and next day He had been.

When I awoke, and looked around,
oh! what a sight to see:
an overflowing box of toys,
especially for me.

This was a day I was allowed
to eat sweets when I liked —
even before my breakfast:
a most unusual sight.

On Christmas Night I would be sad,
because my Dad would say:
"You'll have to wait a whole twelve months,
'till next year's Christmas Day."

REMEMBER THE GOOD TIMES

Rag, Tag and Bobtail, Bill and Ben,
Andy Pandy — but that was then,
The Wooden Tops, and *Picture Book* —
another one, I think, was Look.

Crackerjack, and *Titch and Quackers:*
Basil Brush would drive us crackers.
Dr. Who and *Juke Box Jury;*
Officer Dibble, in a fury.

Magic Roundabout, Lucille Ball;
Z Cars, Arden House on call;
Dr's Finley and *Kildare*
seem to have gone, I don't know where.

Present day programmes aren't the same:
perhaps I am averse to change.
Like life, when it's an open book,
it seems ideal — when back, I look.

THE PLOUGH

When I see stars, my mind recalls
the days when I was young —
the carefree days of childhood,
which, now, seemed so much fun.

On winter nights, my Dad would say,
as soon as it was dark,
"If you look up, you'll see The Plough —
four stars, and then the arc.
And if you follow in a line,
the North Star can be seen,"
alerting me of Christmas days
to come, and that have been.

Each time I look and see The Plough,
the years, they fall away,
and I am standing with my Dad:
it seems like yesterday.

MY MOTHER

My mother is the busy type:
she can't sit still, try as she might.
She seems to have more energy
than all of us, including me.

She packs so much in to one day:
I wish I could do things her way,
But oh, they take me twice as long,
and if done quickly, they go wrong.

My Mum's first love seems to be flowers —
with these she'll while away the hours:
from dawn till dusk she works away
making posies, and bouquets.

Her home is like a magpie's nest,
except not gold, but flowers pressed.
With these she decorates her walls:
it looks just like a stately hall.

Her cross-stitch too, it plays a part —
so beautiful, it is an art.
Her demonstrations take her far:
what luck she has a decent car.

Her house seems full of silver cups:
there must be skill here, not just luck
Together with my Dad you see —
she went and produced — little me.

THE DAIRY HERD

I love to see the dairy herd,
when grazing in the field,
replenishing their grass intake,
to supplement their yield.

They live life at a cautious pace —
you cannot hurry them.
If only we could be the same:
no worries, where, or when.

They do not kindly take to change,
and when things do go wrong,

4

they'll bellow, run, and make a fuss:
a noisy, boisterous throng.

When life is running smoothly,
they are gentle to the core:
they seem to understand the things we say,
and, maybe, more.

With big brown eyes, they look at us,
so trusting in their way;
then give their milk up readily,
at milking-time, each day.

MY HUSBAND

My husband is the type of man
who likes to help out when he can:
neighbours, strangers, in-laws too —
there's nothing he won't try to do.

Farming is his stock-in-trade:
in an office he would fade.
An outdoor life is what suits him —
his face, it always wears a grin.

The children are his pride and joy,
both little girl and older boy.
Since they were born, he has been great,
except that he is always late.

I hope I feature in his life:
his loving, faithful, devoted wife,
who stands her ground, most every day,
and very often gets her way.

An answer I can never get:
he'll joke or clown around, and yet,
if something hurts me, he won't mock —
he's there beside me, like a rock.

I think his heart is big enough
to incorporate all of us – but —
his farm is what takes pride of place,
and, on this note, I rest my case.

PLEASURABLE PAIN

My husband's so annoying —
he drives me up the wall.
I think he tries to wind me up,
to see how far I'll fall.

He asks me to repeat things
I know that he has heard,
and when I do, he'll ask again:
it really is absurd.

He thinks that he is funny —
he does not realise,
that he is getting on my nerves:
and that's not very wise.

When we are watching tele —
especially a soap,
he takes control, wants S4C:*
to him it is a joke.

When we all go to *Bromley's,**
a cushion he demands;
and in the cupboard by the till,
there is one close to hand.

If, when we're at the checkout,
there's a query with the price,
my husband will announce to all
a free gift would be nice.

He talks to perfect strangers —
he's never ill at ease,
whilst we are hoping that the ground
will swallow us up, please.

He's such a jolly person,
and always full of fun:
things never seem to get him down —
he's cheerful like the sun.

He helps me cook the dinner,
on Sundays — when he's free:
he'll wash the dishes, wipe them up —
and even make the tea.

When asked, if I could live
my life again, what would I do?
Of course, I would still marry him —
it's crazy, but it's true.

You see, he is quite harmless,
and treats me very well.
The thought of training someone else
is my idea of hell!

*S4C = Channel 4 Wales   Bromley's = a café in Oswestry

THE NINTENDO

My husband has a Nintendo
on which he often plays.
I think he is addicted:
he's clearly changed his ways.

He used to be reliable:
an all-round, helpful sort.
But now he doesn't listen —
which leaves me overwrought.

If I ask him a favour,
an 'OK' I will get.
But later, when the task's not done,
it's, "You've not asked me yet!"

And if I interrupt him,
a frown I'm bound to see.
His concentration must not wane —
top score it has to be.

It's simply not important,
this electronic game.
I cannot understand him:
He used to be so sane.

I guess I shouldn't grumble,
'cause, elsewhere, he could be.
I think I'll count my blessings:
at least he's here with me.

THE PENCIL

Today Gron* lost a pencil —
he hadn't got a clue.
He turned the office upside down,
but nothing came to view.

The desk had been turned over,
the papers double-checked.
The filing cabinet was not
the culprit, I suspect.

The floor was well inspected;
the bin was rummaged through;
no pencil could be found at all —
so what was he to do?

He told me what had happened.
I started to retrace,
and found the pencil straight away —
inside the pencil-case.

*Gron – Goronwy, Brenda's husband

GRON'S HICCUPS

I'm sure Gron gets the hiccups
just to annoy me.
He cannot have them quietly —
why ever can that be?

They seem to last for ages —
the noise goes on and on.
I say, "Just try to hold your breath —
perhaps they will be gone."

"Try drinking some cold water —
maybe will do the trick.
Please can you think of something else?
Or, find a ball to kick?"

"Perhaps a spoon of sugar? —
Try anything that helps.
If you don't stop this nonsense soon,
I'll strangle you myself."

"I've heard a spoon put down the back,
or scaring you might work.

You have to figure something out,
before I go berserk."

At last, the house is silent:
they've stopped, all on their own.
Please God, if they come back again,
he can quieten down the tone.

EIFION ELIS

Our son, he was born, on a cold winter's day.
What a mad time to have him, some people would say.
He weighed in a healthy seven pounds and thirteen,
but he was two weeks late — oh, where had he been?

The nurses, they were of him, ever so fond:
they called him their 'wonderful strawberry blonde'.
He slept quite a lot, and cried quite a bit:
his stomach, it was like a bottomless pit.

We were so proud of him, first born, I suppose,
so perfect, with ten tiny fingers and toes.
When looking at things, his eyes seemed to bore:
his great-grandma said, "He has been here before."

Today, he's fourteen, and quite the young man:
I wish I could go back to when it began.
But time can't stand still, and he eats like a horse —
he only takes after his father — of course.

THE WILD FLOWER

Our son came over Thursday night
to titivate our lawn:
except the grass had grown so tall,
he could be there till dawn.

The mower had to work so hard
to cope with all the growth,
but Eifion had said he would come:
he'd even pledged his troth.

The only problem was our Pip,
who tried to bite the wheels.
Black rubber seems to drive her mad:
I'm not sure what she feels.
The lawn was mowed, except one patch,

where a wild flower grew.
Our son went round this pretty plant:
it looked so pink and new.

We're not sure what the flower's called,
or how it came to be,
slap-bang in middle of our lawn,
for all the world to see.

I think this proves that our dear son
does have a softer side:
it's there somewhere inside him —
the part he likes to hide.

But every now and then it comes
to light, and then I see,
again, the little boy, who graced
our lives so perfectly.

THE SPRAYER

When my son got up this morning,
he wasn't feeling well:
a few too many, late last night,
was the reason — I can tell.

He cooked himself some bacon
but couldn't stomach that,
so he came here to do some work —
and maybe have a chat.

The aim was to go spraying —
the docks were spreading fast —
but they found there was a problem:
the Sprayer would not last.

The frost had done some damage:
last winter it was cold.
The Sprayer, it was leaking so,
no water would it hold.

There was another problem:
some bits were breaking off.
So they came and had some dinner —
I think they'd had enough.

Replenished they went out again,
to have another go.
They took one of my rubber gloves:
what for, I just don't know.

I heard the tractor engine:
it must have worked a treat.
They are quite good at fixing things —
sometimes, it's quite a feat.

When I asked about the verdict,
my son was quick to say,
"I think I will tomorrow,
put the Sprayer on E-Bay."

AWEL HAF

Our daughter was born
late one summer's eve;
the weather was warm,
and silent the breeze.

She was so perfect
in every small way:
"We can not believe it,"
we heard ourselves say.

She had big, blue eyes,
a small button nose;
with a rosebud-shaped mouth,
she cried out her woes.

She seemed like a doll,
at six pounds and four;
so easy to handle
till when, we're not sure.

Our daughter has made
our life so complete;
our only wish is
that she could be more neat.

Today she is ten.
Where have the years gone?
It seems only yesterday
that she was born.

AWEL

My daughter is a happy soul:
she brightens up the place,
with big blue eyes, and winning smile —
an all-round cheery face.

I miss her when she's not around —
it's like the sun's gone in.
It seems so deathly quiet
that without her, it's a sin.

She chatters all the time, you see.
(Her brother says, 'Too much!')
She's such a friendly, honest girl —
her smile is like a touch.

She has her faults, of course:
she's quite assertive, and she's bossy.
She does not mince her words,
so what she says can't be called 'glossy'.

Her bedroom used to be a mess —
her wardrobe overcrowded.
Since she has had a new clothes rail
her floor's no longer shrouded.

We're all aware when she comes home
our tranquil peace is shattered.
It's "Where's the light? Can I have help?
I'm hungry, and I'm knackered."

She works as a hairdresser,
and has part-time jobs right now.
Her plan is to go mobile —
and she will — she'll show them how.

When she comes home, I never know
what hue her hair will be.
Will it be purple, blue or red?
I'll have to wait and see.

Quite often she comes home from work,
and promptly falls asleep.
She may have been quite busy
but she's had late nights this week.

Since she has passed her driving test
I asked she let me know,
that she's arrived there safely,
wherever she might go.

And sure enough, my loving child —
always the one to please —
gives me three rings on her mobile
to put my mind at ease.

On birthdays, Christmas, Mothers' Day
she'll always find the time,
to make each day a special one,
this thoughtful girl of mine.

When she gets wed and moves away,
to start a brand new home,
I hope she knows I'm always here,
beside the telephone.

I hope she'll often visit me:
she's welcome any time,
because I cannot do without
my daily dose of sunshine.

WAITING

Waiting for the phone to ring —
will my daughter call?
The only sound is silence
from the gadget in the hall.

I make sure I am busy
so that I won't think.
If only she would contact me,
then I would have a link.

At last the phone is ringing —
I rush into the hall:
to hear my daughter's voice so clear,
makes me feel ten feet tall.

HONESTY DOES PAY

The day my daughter found a ring,
we weren't sure what to do.
But honesty won in the end —
and guilt played its part too.

We took it to the local Nick —
were told in voice so deep,
if not reclaimed within one month,
it would be ours to keep.

And so today we had a call:
the owners of the ring,
they were so pleased to get it back,
and wondered what to bring.

When they arrived, it was to thank
my daughter, and to make
her day complete, by giving her
some money and a cake.

Considering the week gone by,
and what's occurred today,
I'm sure you will agree with me
that honesty *does* pay.

TOYS

I've often wondered what if,
when I close the Nursery door,
the toys all come alive, and play:
the lion, he would roar.

The dolls could have a tea-party —
with games, if they were good.
I'm sure the bears would rather have
a picnic in the wood.

Helen the clown could make them laugh,
performing funny tricks.
Snoopy the dog would run around,
retrieving far-thrown sticks.

Mary the doll would cry,
until someone patted her back.
If Bump the elephant got hurt
his trunk I'm sure he'd pack.

And if they all played Hide and Seek,
an answer I would get,
to *why* my daughter's toys are not found,
where they *should* be kept.

A MOTHER'S LOVE

A mother's love towards her child
is something quite unique:
you'll never find its equal,
no matter where you seek.

It seems to stem from early on,
whilst growing in the womb,
knowing there is a child in there
that you will see quite soon.

The first time that you feel it kick
is a momentous day:
it won't be long before it's here,
once it is on its way.
When they first give your child to you,
and place it in your arms,
you'll do your very best to see
it's kept away from harm.

And as they grow you'll want to keep
them always by your side.
You'll be afraid to let them face
the world so big and wide.

But let them go you have to do,
when they are tall and strong.
To keep them close and tied to you
would be so very wrong.

When you finally cut the cord,
you hope they won't go far,
and that the distance between you
is possible by car.

A mother then can only hope
when they have flown the nest,
that they reciprocate her love,
and try their very best.

MY MOTHER-IN-LAW

My mother-in-law is someone
who will rally round you,
if you're ill.
Her care and compassion
is equalled by few:
she's always so helpful —
but that's nothing new.
She likes to feel needed,
of that there's no doubt:
it's really no trouble
to help someone out.
She's always out walking,
with *somebody's* dog —
some people consider –
it's her job.

If somebody wants something
quick from the shops,
whatever the weather,
outside she will pop.
She's always performing
a neighbourly task,
it's never a problem — you just have to ask.
Today she's eighty, and so full of fun.
She's ever so busy,
and really quite young.
It's known she's knitted
the odd pair of gloves:
she's the type of woman
everyone loves.

SMOKEY, BANDIT and PIP

Since we have had Smokey and Bandit and Pip,
have our lives improved? Yes, I think, quite a bit.
Smokey's the shy one, she loves to be fussed:
she rubs in our legs, and then rolls in the dust.

Pip loves to chase Smokey, and wants her to play,
but Smokey won't have it, she just runs away.
Smokey is out when the farm's gone to bed.
She'll run to meet Gron coming down from the shed.

Gron lifts her up, and together they play.
Then Gron will put Smokey to sleep in the hay.
Bandit's the bold one, with Eifion he chats;
he climbs on his shoulders, and sits on his cap.

He'll play with Pip, but Pip pulls at his ears:
Bandit will tolerate this with no fears.
Pip will drag Bandit along by his fur:
Bandit's quite happy — he might even purr.

As far as our black cat goes, Pip's met her match:
he dislikes this boisterous black pup on his patch.
He'll spit at Pip, and so Pip stays away:
she'll bark from a distance, but won't try to play.

Our Neli has taken to Pip very well.
What Neli is thinking, God knows — who can tell?
They play-fight, and often play tag on the lawn:
if we let them they'd be there from dusk until dawn.

But Neli is boss, and Pip knows her place:
a look of disgust can be seen on Nel's face,
when Pip carries off silage net, and the string,
wellies, screwdrivers, in fact anything.

Pip loves to see people, she wriggles about:
I'm almost afraid that she'll turn inside out.
When Awel comes home, and she opens her door,
Pip gets so excited she pees on the floor.

When my thoughts return to when Pip first arrived —
that little pink bow round her neck, well attired,
we all fell in love with this puppy, so sweet,
with ears that flop forwards, and little brown feet.

So, thank you the Mountfords, for all of your gifts,
for Smokey — and Bandit — and cute little Pip.

SMOKEY'S OP

Smokey had an op today,
a visit to the Vet,
to have her ovaries removed
and uterus, I'll bet.

Awel said she'd take her there:
a cardboard box was found.
But Smokey wouldn't stay inside:
she likes to run around.

She sat on Awel's shoulders,
whilst travelling in the car,
it's just as well the journey
to the Vet was not that far.

I rang the Vet at half past two:
they said collect at four.
So Gron and me went there this time,
but when we reached the door,
a nurse came out to tell us
that our kitten was OK.

But as they'd put her in the box
her temper was quite frayed.
That was an understatement —
a downright lie in fact.
She spat, and hissed, and scratched poor Gron:
she'd not an ounce of tact.

So in the car we let her out
She lay down on Gron's cap.
I guess that after her ordeal
all she wanted was a nap.

When we came home she settled
in the garage to recover:
she had two stitches in her side —
a patch without fur cover.

She had warm milk, a little food —
a meal that was quite light.
By nine o'clock she seemed quite well,
and settled for the night.

Next day she was allowed outside
But much to our dismay,
She'd poo'd in the potato box
We threw the lot away.

Next week she has her stitches out
But this time we will know,
To leave her loose inside the car
Quite happily she'll go.

Smokey will not have kittens
Of motherhood she's free,
But now she's lost her ovaries
will she need HRT*?

*HRT =Hormone Replacement Therapy

BANDIT

This morning, it was Bandit's turn
to visit local Vet,
a damaged eye to be removed:
a fight last night, I'll bet.

He looked so sorry for himself —
a lethargic scrap of fur.
He clung to Gron whilst in the car:
despite all, he did purr.

When Karen took a look at him,
she saw he was well tooled.
"I'll whip his balls out now he's here —
his ardour will be cooled!"

They gave him bed and breakfast;
then Awel brought him home:
his eye was stitched, his balls removed,
around his head, a cone.

The trouble was, whilst travelling home,
he peed in Awel's car:
he must have been quite desperate,
plus feeling below par.

We popped him in the rabbit hutch,
while Awel cleaned her seat.
The smell was strong so Awel said,
"Febreze will make things sweet."

Meanwhile, our other cats were keen
to get inside the car:
the pungent smell attracted them —
they might come from afar.

Two pills a day he had to take
infection to prevent:
we had to crush them in his food —
palaver —though well meant.

The pills were labelled Bandit Jones:
the name made us smile.
I hoped this episode would teach,
'No fighting for a while.'

Vet's bill was one hundred pounds —
much more than we had thought.
But we were glad to have him back —
a lesson had been taught.

I really thought he'd not return
from visit to the Vet.
We love him dearly — he is ours:
a most mischievous pet.

BANDIT'S THOUGHTS

Why won't that woman let me in?
It's very cold out here.
I'm sitting on the windowsill,
Through which I can but peer.

She lets me in when weather's fine,
'cause then my feet are clean.
But when it's raining cats and dogs,
she's really very mean.

When Awel's home, she wipes my feet,
then I am allowed in —

but only if I sit upon
a towel: it's a sin!

If I am good, Awel will let
me sit upon her lap.
I'll purr away, and curl up tight.
Then I might have a nap.

I can stay in if I behave,
But sometimes I can-not:
if I smell fish, or sausages,
I just don't give a jot.

I'll jump up on the draining-board
and eat whatever's there.
If Gron sees me I get a clout —
I'll wear my icy stare.

I'm bundled out without a care —
I know what I've done wrong.
I guess I shouldn't push my luck —
I wasn't in for long.

At feeding time I'm always there,
but so is Pip the dog.
She gets excited, barks a lot,
and jumps just like a frog.

Sometimes she drags me round the yard,
in playful mood, of course.
She'll pull my ears and tail, but she's
quite wary of my claws.

If she slips up, or goes too far,
a scratch is what she'll get.
She knows how far to push me but
I'll get the critter yet.

On other days, Pip is my friend:
we'll chill out in the sun.
She can be good, if she but try —
I know it can be done.

But cats and dogs aren't meant to be
good friends — it's not deemed cool.
So, Pip and me, will always be
'Exception to the Rule'.

BANDIT THINKS AGAIN

Oh God, she's got that cup again:
I burnt my tongue last time.
I only had a little sip —
to me it was a crime.

The cup was on the windowsill,
I strained to have a look,
I stuck my tongue in, but it was hot:
it was a risk I took.

My little tongue was sore for days,
I do remember that,
but I am quite inquisitive —
an all-round nosey cat.

It think it's tea that's in the cup:
I guess it's really nice,
'cause if it wasn't, she would not
drink it at any price.

One day I'll pluck up courage
to try my luck again.
But until then, I'll bide my time,
and stay away from pain.

PIP'S THOUGHTS

Oh, come on Gron, I want to go:
you're in the house too long.
I could go off all by myself,
but I know that would be wrong.

If you leave the back door open,
I'll creep in on the mat.
I'll talk to you, and wag my tail —
just for a friendly pat.

I know I'm not allowed inside —
not like that wretched cat.
He comes and goes just as he likes —
I don't agree with that.

At last you're here, and off we go.
What will we do today?
Is it the bike, or catching moles?
I don't mind either way.

You fetch the bike and I jump on:
I lean against your back.
I feel quite safe if I do this —
I think I've learnt the knack.

We end up in the meadow;
there is a wood nearby.
You won't see me for quite a while:
my spirit's soaring high.

In the wood, there's smells of every kind
to keep me occupied:
there's foxes, badgers, squirrels too —
they make me quite pie-eyed.

At suppertime I eat my food,
but can't bear to go in:
since we have lost poor Neli,
I create quite a din.

You see, her ghost is always there —
it scares me, and I bark.
Or maybe I will chew my way
outside when it is dark.

The sensor light is often on
'cause I am on the prowl.
If I see something I dislike,
I'll warn you with a growl.

These days I am allowed to come
and go, just as I please:
if I can see you in the house,
then I am quite at ease.

THE SPIDER

I live in a hole, that's sombre and small,
behind the cupboard, so close to the wall.
I venture out, when the household is still,
scaring nobody, and causing no ill.

Some folk are scared of me, I don't know why:
I cannot harm them, I watch from on high.
My web is too fine to cause them much trouble:
sharp gust of wind, it bursts like a bubble.

I spin my web with careful precision:
It's easy once I've made my decision,
I can only hope that the housewife so tall
will not get the duster, and ruin it all.

All of a sudden a juicy fat fly
lands on the cupboard — I daren't blink an eye.
His buzz turns to panic: he's trapped in my web.
I move so suddenly: then he is dead.

When I've completed my meal, and I'm full,
I start to charge about, like a small bull,
repairing my web until it looks like new.
Will I catch more flies today? Maybe a few.

ARACHNOPHOBIA

Each time I venture up the stairs,
one thought is in my mind:
will there be one of them up here?
Who knows what I might find.

There seem to be a lot this year:
I blame the summer sun.
Maybe the warm and sultry nights
gave vent to creature fun.

The bathroom is their main domain —
they lurk inside the bath,
How do they get there? I don't know:
have they a secret path?

I know they will not harm me,
but they move so rapidly:
arachnid presence is well known
to make some people flee.

The large ones look quite scary,
and their legs extremely long,
but harming them is not my way:
that would seem very wrong.

They are shy creatures, and I'm sure
quite terrified of us.
So, why on earth do humans scream,
and create such a fuss?

THE MOTH

Where do the moths come from at night?
Where are they in the day?
Is it they're nocturnal?
It clearly looks that way.

If you go out in summer sun,
there's not one to be seen,
but surely they are somewhere?
They always seem so keen.

Perhaps they fly up to the sun
at hottest time midday,
then like fictitious Icarus
their wings are burnt away.

But soon as daylight starts to wane
to warn you of the night,
a moth comes out of God knows where,
to fly around the light.

Their actions are repetitive:
they just fly round and round,
until they crash into the light,
and fall down to the ground.

Why do they act so stupidly?
Why are there moths at all?
Existence seems so futile,
when pride comes, before a fall.

THE PET LAMB

I am afraid I've lost my mum:
I feel quite hollow in my tum.
My mum died there beneath that tree,
which meant there was no milk for me.

The farmer came and took me in.
I think I made an awful din,
He put me in a little shed
where, grudgingly, I made my bed.

He bottle-fed me every day
and then I rested in the hay.
A mother's milk is hard to beat:
I did not like the rubber teat.

When he was sure I'd not go far
The farmer left the door ajar.
I'd follow him around the farm,
But most of all I loved the barn.
In here were calves who'd say, "Hello":
a friendly face is nice to know.

The children like to play with me:
I'm grateful for their company.
They have a rabbit who will come
and talk to me if I feel glum.

I'd like to go back to my friends.
When that will be, I think depends
on when I start to eat the grass.
But, oh, how slowly time does pass.

I hear my friends out on the hill.
I wish that I was with them still:
They gambol, play and run about.
When watching them I feel left out.

But when the rain is lashing down,
and everybody wears a frown,
I'm thankful for my little shed,
where I am warm, and dry, and fed.

THE BIG CAT

Whilst motoring along the road,
my daughter at my side,
it never once occurred to me
that we might need to hide.

It was quite dark. I felt a thud.
I glanced into the mirror.
What I saw there fair made me jump:
I felt an icy shiver.

For what I saw, I'll not forget:
it had a cat-like face.
I've never seen the like before:
what species, or what race?

It seemed to be as tall as me,
its paws against the car.
I didn't stop, I carried on:
I wanted to go far.

My daughter had seen nothing,
nor felt the creature's leap,
which made me wonder
if I'd been dreaming in my sleep.

On close inspection of the car,
large paw-marks could be seen.
There had been something there that night,
but what could it have been?

FARMING MATTERS

EDWINA

1988

How dare Edwina Currie
rake up the past like this?
Does she not realise the hurt,
and rift, in wedded bliss.

John Major made a big mistake
so many years ago,
if Norma could forgive him then,
what else is there to know?

Because she wants to sell her book
she thinks it's quite OK
to publicise these private facts:
I hope she's made to pay.

I think she's quite disgraceful:
forgiveness she should beg.
As someone said to me today,
'Edwina's a bad egg.'

THE BEEF CRISIS

April 1996

Will it be safe, or will it not,
to eat the beef that we have got?
The Government has been so slow
in showing us which way to go.

For British beef is banned abroad,
which will leave us with quite a hoard,
and what are we supposed to do
with pounds of rotting, excess, moo?

What I don't understand is how
infected sheep were fed to cows.
We know that cows eat mainly grass:
this stupid action must be crass.

They have no proof that CJD
is caught from cows with BSE.

This circumstantial evidence
to angry farmers, makes no sense.

In farming, suicides are high.
It seems a selfish way to die,
but all this stress may take its toll,
on some poor unsuspecting soul.

For many people it's too late:
their jobs have gone — how they must hate
the people up above, who wait
for two years, and then speculate.

As time goes on, things will improve:
beef will again be on the move.
This crisis will seem years away,
until another one – some day.

*CJD – Creutzfeldt-Jacob disease; B.S.E. Bovine Spongiform Encephalopathy

THE FOOT AND MOUTH CRISIS
2001

What's going on? Has Britain gone completely barking mad,
slaughtering its livestock, as if all of it is bad?
They're killing uninfected stock without a second thought:
the herd you built up from scratch, no way can that be bought.
The air is filled with burning flesh, the sky's a smoky haze:
you do your best to blot it out — your mind is in a daze.
Who is to blame for this attack on farmers, yet again?
Not just content with BSE, 'They' have to cause more pain.
By 'They', I mean the Government, the suited men down South:
They haven't got a bloody clue; They go by word of mouth.
They sit there in their offices, completely unaware
of all the havoc that they wreak. I wonder, do They care?
The Election changed all: Blair said the scourge had gone.
He opened up the footpaths. How could he have been so wrong?
Of course, the Foot and Mouth came back, to some parts anyway.
When will Blair and his army stop, and hear what farmers say?
Now eight months on, things seem to have abated, but of course
we farmers aren't complacent, for They haven't found the source.
Does it lie dormant in some sheep? They would be to blame
if it re-infected our herds — now that would be a shame.
Let us hope the Government has learnt from all of this,
and from now on, we farmers can enjoy 'a life of bliss'!

THE A.I. COMETH
(Artificial Inseminator)

Why won't the farmer let me out,
to graze with all my friends?
What has he got in store for me?
To Market, some, he sends.

I do not have to wait too long —
a car pulls up outside.
A man comes in, all plastic clad:
I want to run and hide.

He marches up, this space-like man —
his arm goes up my bum.
'Undignified' is how I feel —
it's certainly no fun.

I'm glad to say it doesn't last
too long, this strange ordeal.
No sooner has he come — he's gone —
my mind begins to reel.

Have I been raped? I am not sure.
I wish we had a bull.
My dignity would be intact —
there's room here: we're not full.

I'm sure my friends will join me
in campaigning for a mate.
If we'd a bull, we could go out
upon a proper date.

TO WHOM IT MAY CONCERN

Who is it stealing farmers' bikes,
at this most busy time?
Why not be like the rest of us,
and learn to toe the line?

Were you not taught the difference
between what's right and wrong?
How dare you come and take what's ours,
and sell it for a song?

What makes you think you have the right
to take what is not yours?
If you'd been brought up properly,
you'd work by doing chores.

You can't go on behaving
in such a criminal way.
The time will come when you get caught,
and then you'll have to pay.

You'll take one bike too many,
and be punished for your crime.
My hope is that you won't be fined,
but end up doing Time.

FERTILIZER

When Gron ordered fertilizer
from John Lewis, he was told,
'Try the Polish one, it's cheaper,'
so the order, it was sold.

When time came, the driver called us
to explain that he was lost;
he was Polish: "No speak English,"
we discovered to our cost.

He just wanted Gron to meet him,
but our post code, it was wrong.
He kept saying, "I'm in Church Lane,"
then the signal, it was gone.

In the end Gron went to meet him:
his Sat Nav had brought him here.
They unloaded very quickly,
but a problem became clear.

He kept asking, "Where is exit?"
He did not like turning round.
In the end they went to Rhiwlas,
Gron, the driver, and our hound.

In the meantime Awel called me,
she could not drive into yard,
Gron had left his tractor open,
and no one was left on guard.

She thought Gron had collapsed nearby,
or run over Pip, our hound.
When she realised what had happened,
great relief was felt all round.

So next time, John Lewis, listen,
don't give us a Polish driver:
they don't understand our lingo —
and they can't say 'fertilizer'.

THE NEW BULK TANK

When we replaced our old bulk tank,
the men were so excited:
they weren't to know that by that night
their feelings would be blighted.

We could not get the milk to cool
down to the right degree:
the tanker had to come here twice —
on Sunday too, poor Tony!

The agitator would not turn:
it fell into the liquid.
The men who put the tank in,
were they rash, or just plain stupid?

The tank wash cycle would not work:
it seems the fuse was feeble.
I half expected he'd turn up —
the famous Mr Beadle*.

During this week I've learnt new words
like 'trip fuse', and 'compressor'.
I don't know what on earth they are —
I'm not a Yale professor.

Now that we have a bigger tank,
and some things still aren't working,
I wish someone had told us
that these problems would be lurking.

*Jeremy Beadle in *Beadle's About*

FROM CLWYD TO POWYS

Since we have changed to Powys,
what has happened to our roads?
The early ice and snow
has only added to our load.
Last year when things were very bad
the gritter came each day.
This year, we've only seen it twice.
Surely, that's not the way?

We have to take our children down
to meet the old school bus.
The driver claims he can't get up the hills
without a fuss.
The Government is spending more (I've heard),
on education.
If we can't get our kids to school,
no cause for celebration,

My husband's had to tow the Milk Marque truck
up icy banks.
We've now had heaps of salt and for that reason
we give thanks.
But what we really want is frequent gritting to remove
the ice rink that's our roads,
to keep us on the move,
We'll not refuse the snowplough,
when we're under several feet.
The Council's help on days like these
is very hard to beat.

So, Councillors of Powys, who live near Llandrindod Wells,
give us a thought,
the people who live north:
near the Berwyn Fells.

IN THE NEWS
BEN NEEDHAM

who went missing in 1992

When young Ben Needham disappeared on the Greek Isle of Kos,
his family knew how it felt to suffer a great loss.
His mother, she was out at work, his father had come home,
which meant his grandparents were left to see to him alone.

When first they realised Ben was not where he was meant to be,
they searched the well, and land, as far as naked eye could see.
The family were once accused of harming little Ben,
but the Police soon realised that it could not be them.

Poor Ben was only twenty months when this nightmare occurred:
to family and friends, reality was blurred?
As time went on abduction seemed to be the only way
a child could disappear, and not be sighted since that day.

In Greece there is a racket, whereby children can be sold
on the black market, for many pounds, I'm told.
The family, of course, were panic-stricken at this time:
they could not understand who would be guilty of this crime.

The grandparents felt they were responsible for Ben.
The guilt they felt would be immense: my heart goes out to them.
Ben's mother tried to take her life; she did not want to live.
She now has a young daughter, who has so much love to give.

Of course, Ben's always on her mind — she only wants him back.
She'd like to know he's safe, but signs of hope she lacks.
By now, Ben would be six or seven, a blonde-haired, blue-eyed boy.
If he were found, his family would celebrate with joy.

But would they recognise the boy that Ben has now become?
And if they did, would he believe that he was their young son?
He might not speak our language, and be happy where he is.
Would it be fair to uproot him, from folk he sees as his?

The situation is, I'm sure, so hard to tolerate,
I hope they find Ben safe and well, before it is too late.
The family have suffered, with their health under the strain:
I think they are remarkable, to cope with so much pain.
Ben's grandparents go back to Kos, when meagre funds allow.
They won't give up: they'll find out who took Ben, and why, some-how.

CÉLINE FIGARD

1996

(IF ONLY)

Last year Britain had a visit
from a French girl so naïve.
She intended to spend Christmas
with a cousin, I believe.

When she got here she decided
that hitchhiking she would go.
So she got into a lorry
with a man she did not know.

When they found her ten days later
she no longer felt the cold.
And her father, when he saw her,
changed from young to very old.

Two months later they had found him
and his white Mercedes truck.
I am glad the world is safer
and that he ran out of luck.

The Police have been punctilious,
finding out who was to blame.
But for Céline's loving parents
life will never be the same.

They must think of mainland Britain
as a cold, unpleasant place,
and their memories of Christmas
will be haunted by her face.

I do hope they will be able
as time passes, to find peace.
Though I'm sure the words *'If Only'*
will, in their minds, never cease.

DUNBLANE

1996

One cold and breezy winter's morn
a madman made his way,
into a Scottish Junior School —
armed with four guns, they say.

He opened fire in the Gym,
where infants played care-free
and killed sixteen of them in all,
and, teacher, brutally.

He must have planned what he would do
upon that fateful day,
because he went and shot himself:
it was the only way.

The dismayed people of Dunblane
could not believe their eyes —
that someone could behave like that,
and wreck so many lives.

The question everyone has asked,
is why did this take place?
I don't suppose we'll ever know —
but what a wicked waste!

The world is out in mourning,
for the people of Dunblane.
Life may return to 'normal' —
but will never be the same.

WHY?

Why does it seem, when things go wrong,
the world is at an end?
Or when you've finished a good book
that you have lost a friend?

Why does a problem seem less big
when shared with someone close?
Why does sad music from a film
make people feel morose?

Why does the grass smell clean and fresh
when thunderstorms have passed?
Why do the flowers bloom again,
and years fly by so fast?

Why does the snow fall silently
to make a perfect world,
but then is spoiled, immediately,
by rubbish that is hurled?

Why do so many people die
from illnesses they've caught?
Why were the children of Dunblane
wiped out without a thought?

Most people have a cross to bear —
a problem in their life.
Why can't we wave a magic wand,
and banish all the strife?

DIANA

1997

The day Diana passed away,
the sky remained a murky grey.
I wonder, did it sense our loss,
and know the world had lost its gloss?

When she became a royal bride,
her fame spread fast: it was worldwide.
And when her handsome sons were born,
we did not think that soon we'd mourn.

The clothes she wore were much admired.
Of charities she never tired.
Victims of AIDS — she was the one
who held their hands, and did not run.

The landmines issue is a cause
on which she wanted brand new laws.
To ban them all was her desire.
This problem, in her mind, was dire.

The children were her main concern,
and with her guidance they would learn,
the normal things, like love and fun,
I wonder, will these now be done?

She loved young children everywhere.
It is a gift to show you care:
a smile, a touch, a gentle word.
To think she's gone is just absurd.

Three things about her funeral
in my mind made it beautiful:
a fitting song, a brother's speech,
a wreath that made you want to weep.

Diana's life was not in vain:
she was like sunshine in the rain.
I'm sure she'd want us all to sing,
for she gave us our future king.

SARAH PAYNE

2001

What kind of monster takes a child,
abuses her, and then,
discards her body in a field.
What is wrong with these men?

They're paedophiles, or so they say,
so what does all this mean?
It's children they prefer, I've heard,
on women they're not keen.

The paedophile is of the view
they do nothing wrong,
I cannot understand this
when a little girl is gone.

The parents, what must they go through?
Imagine how they'd feel,
just thinking what he'd done to her:
their worst nightmare is real.

But on the other hand of course
my heart goes out to her,
the mother of the paedophile:
her mind must be a blur.

Her son is now a murderer:
she cannot understand,
how someone she gave birth to
is now sought throughout the land.

There is no happy outcome
to conclude this sorry tale.
The paedophile got life this time:
so many years in jail.

The little girl they've grown to know
and love is gone for good.
How dare this person end her life:
be punished? 'Course he should.

HOLLY WELLS AND JESSICA CHAPMAN

2002

If someone takes your child away,
what anguish you would feel.
You might think, "I will wake up soon —
this nightmare is unreal."
But for two little ten-year-olds
this really did come true.
They disappeared, without a trace —
which baffled me and you.

The families of Jessica
and Holly must have prayed
their daughters be returned to them—
their sorrow be allayed.
But in due course, to their dismay,
two bodies came to light:
a woman, walking her dog that day,
observed that dreadful sight.

A man was soon arrested
upon a murder charge.
His name was Ian Huntley,
and his girlfriend, Maxine Carr.
He worked at Soham College,
as a janitor, no less.
She'd taught the little ten-year-olds,
who trusted them, I guess.

The residents of Soham
must be shocked beyond belief,
that someone from amongst their midst
could cause them so much grief.
Perverting course of justice
was the charge for Maxine Carr.
But, as for Ian Huntley,
they could not proceed that far.

Apparently he's claiming now
he's mentally insane.
If this is proved, he won't stand trial —
eternally a bane.

MADELEINE McCANN

who went missing on 3rd May, 2007

Where are you, Madeleine McCann?
The search has been in vain.
Your disappearance from this world
has caused us so much pain.

Your parents Kate and Gerry
must have strength with which to cope.
If only they could have a sign
to give them new-found hope.

It seems the Portuguese police
were wrong when they accused
your parents of this dreadful crime:
they must have felt abused.

It's surely bad enough to lose
a daughter in this way,
without being told that it was you,
who was to blame, that day.

Poor Madeleine was only three,
when taken from her bed.
I hope that she's alive and well:
the other can't be said.

I hope she's being cared for,
by someone who's good and kind,
and that she's happy as can be,
for her own peace of mind.

I wonder if, in years to come,
a memory will stir.
Will she remember something small,
or will it be a blur?

As for Kate and Gerry,
their life-sentence will go on:
they'll not forget a daughter,
who was there, and then was gone.

JADE

22nd March, 2009

Jade Goody touched the hearts of millions
sympathetic to her plight:
she was one of life's survivors,
till she lost the will to fight.

She discovered fame and fortune
on *Big Brother* I believe.
She was not what you'd call brainy,
and perhaps she was naive.

Cervical cancer is a killer
if it's not stopped in its tracks:
it must not be left untreated —
these are plain and simple facts.

She got married in the spotlight,
raising money for her boys.
Then I think all three were christened:
she showed elegance and poise.

She did not deserve to suffer:
twenty seven's so young to die.
Two small boys without a mother —
father Jack will get them by.

On Mother's Day it had to happen:
in her sleep Jade passed away,
Two small cards were left unopened —
a symbolic, poignant day.

So let this be a lesson, ladies —
Jade must not have died in vain.
Get your symptoms treated early,
and prevent yourselves this pain.

MICHAEL JACKSON

1958-2009

Michael Jackson was just fifty,
when he passed away:
a young man in his prime,
until that fateful day.

He shot to fame whilst very young —
perhaps too young, in fact.
He didn't have a childhood:
how do you cope with that?

His life seemed fraught with problems.
Perhaps he made mistakes.
But we all do that, don't we?
Why not give him a break?

He seemed to be a troubled soul,
this legend, King of Pop.
His generous and caring ways
helped get him to the top.

Some unkind people found a fault
with all that he achieved.
They'll sing his praises now he's gone —
harsh hypocrites indeed.

I think he was misunderstood:
some thought him very strange.
But we're all different, aren't we,
(and perhaps averse to change?)

I wonder if he thought he'd gone
as far as he could go.
There is no answer is there?
I guess we'll never know.

I hope that he has now found peace,
is looking down on us.
I think he would be quite amazed
at seeing all the fuss.

He will go down in history —
a genius gone too soon.
I think we'll all remember
the twenty fifth of June.

43

HENRY ALLINGHAM

1896-2009

Henry Allingham, what a life!
One hundred and thirteen years.
What is it like, I wonder,
to outlive all your peers?

He was a World War Veteran —
the First World War in fact.
"Wars are a total waste of time,"
said Henry, mind intact.

When asked the secret of his years,
he answered, with a grin,
"It's cigarettes and whiskey,"
and, oh yes, "Wild, wild women."

He used to go around the schools
with tales of his adventures.
He told the children to be good:
let's hope he touched their senses.

A great, great, great granddad —
not a goal most men achieve.
That's six generations:
not easy to believe.

Prince Charles said of him,
"He was one of our nation's 'Historic Treasures'."
I'm sure these words describe him well —
he's not one for half-measures.

He was the sole survivor
of the Jutland war, I've read.
How many of us could cope with
so many comrades dead?

He was in the Royal Navy,
and the RAF.
He lost his sight,
but he was never destined to be deaf.

For one month he was verified
as the world's oldest man.
He survived two World Wars:
beat that, if you can!

HOBBYHORSES

THE POLTERGEIST

The other day I washed my hair,
but something was amiss:
when I turned on hot water tap,
someone had been remiss.

'Cause out of this hot water tap,
cold water poured with force:
I thought that I was losing it —
dementia-bound, of course.

I tried to run cold water,
and sure enough, you've guessed,
hot water poured with gusto:
well, by now I was quite stressed.

So, later on, I asked dear Gron
if he had been at play.
"Oh yes," he said, "I swapped them round —
the names stay on — that way."

Thing was, he said, he'd swapped them round,
for fun, some weeks before:
I simply hadn't noticed,
I'm not sharp-eyed any more.

So now I must remember,
if things don't seem quite right,
it's Gron who's acting poltergeist —
to give us all a fright.

THE RADIATOR SCREW

The bathroom radiator
was stone cold, instead of hot.
It needed bleeding, so I used
the key that I had got.

I'd done this many times before,
but now I was at fault:
I turned the key too far, and so
the bleed screw, it came out.

I couldn't stop the water,
and I lost the bleeding screw.
I panicked, and I ran downstairs,
not sure what I should do.

To my dismay I realised
the water had come through
the ceiling in the kitchen,
the hall, and downstairs loo.

I thought, "I'll turn the stop tap off —
should help to stem the flow."
This act did not help things at all,
but I had to have a go.

By now my husband had arrived,
and said, in voice so terse:
"You've turned the stop tap the wrong way —
you're making matters worse!"

Eventually I found the screw,
so it was put back in
the radiator so the heat
could permeate within.

In future, I won't try to bleed
the bathroom radiator.
My husband can, and, if not now,
I'm sure he'll do it, later.

FRUIT COCKTAIL

Why is it, when I buy a tin
of fruit, it's mainly pears?
Fruit Cocktail's on the label —
I'm not just splitting hairs.

There is one cherry, cut in half;
pineapple — piece, or two;
some peaches, but not many:
and two grapes come into view.

But even then, the pears have bits
that need to be cut off.
They're hard bits from the middle,
that you won't want to scoff.

So, listen, Cocktail Makers,
this simply will not do:
your customers will fade away —
to buy from pastures new.

When I make up a trifle
I want for there to be
a good selection of the fruit
I can present for tea.

I think I will, in future,
prepare my own fresh fruit:
my trifle will be all home-made —
and healthier, to boot.

THE CAR

Why is it, when I'm in a rush,
the blooming car won't start?
I think I might be better off
with Dobbin and his cart.

I turn the key, but not a sound
is heard to ease my mind.
I could lift up hood, but then
who knows what I might find?

The tangled mass of wires
are a labyrinth to me:
I cannot tell if there's a fault —
my eye's not trained to see.

I guess I'm lucky that I have
a husband who does know
just what to do when things go wrong:
to keep me on the go.

NEW SHOES

Gron hates it when I buy new shoes,
'cause he just can't abide
the time I take in choosing them —
although he has retired.

He'll come into the shop, and sit,
reluctantly, to wait
till I've have made my mind up:
he knows we will be late.

He'll ask the Girls what time they close,
and if they will provide,
the Bed and Breakfast he will need
if I just can't decide.

But shoes are so expensive,
they have to be just right:
it's no good if they are too big,
or if they are too tight.

I tend to rearrange the shop,
so many do I try.
There's different colours, types and styles —
the Girls are on stand-by.

My feet are narrow, so I need
a shoe that won't slip off.
Some styles I will eliminate,
but still Gron has to scoff.

Eventually I'm down to two —
which pair I just don't know.

The Girl says, "Why not take them both?"
and I agree, "Righto."

You see, I can return both pairs
unworn, within four weeks.
The Girls at Clarks are very fair:
they know that I'm unique.

PLANET ZOP

Why can't we reach our local banks
by telephone these days?
Your call, it goes to India,
or Scotland, but not Wales.

They say your Branch will call you up
'as soon as they are free'.
You wait, but they don't ring you back
for two days, maybe three.

So what about the elderly
the housebound or the meek?
Some people can't get into town —
they're busy in the week.

At weekends all the banks are closed —
well, our bank anyway.
They have to have their two-day break:
it's progress, so they say.

When I worked in a rival bank,
as secretary, I dealt
efficiciently with all the calls —
at least, that's how I felt.

So what has happened to the girls
who worked alongside me?
They've been replaced by robots
who can't speak, or make the tea.

There are machines for statements,
and paying money in;
in fact, machines for everything,
as long as you've your PIN.

There are machines that give you cash,
but please be on your guard:
you must not hesitate too long,
or they could eat your card.

Try *Banking on the Internet* —
why not liaise with that?
But it's not for the elderly —
they like someone to chat.

So, who is in our banks right now —
I think it's gone to pot.
Perhaps we've been invaded
by aliens from Planet Zop.

Whatever's happened to our banks —
an improvement it is not.
But I guess we'll learn to tolerate —
put up with what we've got.

THE DENTIST'S CHAIR

The chair some people fear the most,
is not on *Mastermind*.
To give that chair this stigma,
would be, I think, unkind.

Few people will sit willingly
upon its leather seat.
The comfy armchair in your home
is very hard to beat.

The chair I am referring to
is one we see each year.
Some people are not scared of it,
whilst others live in fear.

If you can summon up the nerve
to sit down and relax,
someone will come and see to you —
you only have to ask.

The chair will slowly elevate;
a man stands at your side.
And then your fear intensifies
when he says "Open Wide."

THE WASSAILING EVENING

When Hazel asked me, if I'd play
the piano in the Hall,
my first thought was to say, "I can't —
I haven't got the gall,"
But she had asked so nicely
I couldn't let her down.
First I'd need a carol book:
I journeyed into town.

My daughter Awel said
that she would play the harp and sing:
she's so enthusiastic
about almost everything.
The next few weeks we practised
until we were satisfied.
I knew we'd not be perfect
but at least we would've tried.

The Wassailing Night arrived:
Gron was to be Compere.
7.30 was the start:
thank God, not many there.
I think the evening went quite well.
'Course Awel had great fun:
she played the piano, harp, and sang
much better than her mum.
Half way through the proceedings
we had mulled wine and mince pies:
the second half
was better in our eyes.
What made the evening pleasant
was the friendliness of folk:
they made us feel so welcome,
and acknowledged every joke.

Despite all misgivings
I'd had before that night,
the audience sitting in the Hall
dispelled all my stage fright.

RHYDYCROESAU LADIES' GUILD

When Hazel asked me if I'd come
and speak to Ladies' Guild,
I don't think she realised,
I was so strong-willed.

My answer was, "Of course I'll come,
Can I request a chair?"
She said, "That's not a problem:
there are plenty of them there."

By half past seven that Thursday
I drove down in the car.
It didn't take me very long —
Rhydycroesau's not that far.

I think I was quite nervous —
my poems are, you see,
an extension of my inner self:
they are a part of me.

But when I started reading
my nerves were kept at bay.
They even made some choice requests,
which took my breath away.

They made me feel so welcome
that I felt quite at ease:
they're such an honest, friendly group —
not difficult to please.

At the end of the evening,
we had some tea and cakes:
they're obviously good cooks down there —
of that there's no mistake.

Before going home we chatted
'bout all the local news.
It was quite interesting,
but we did mind our p's and q's.

Don't buy a local paper:
you'll surely be fulfilled,
if you go to Rhydycroesau —
and join the Ladies' Guild.

SKID'S LINE DANCING CLASS

I've started to go Line Dancing,
on Monday afternoons.
But it's addictive, so you see
Tuesday can't come too soon.

'Skid' is the one who teaches us.
He's always very smart —
and when he wears his cowboy hat,
he really looks the part.

Some of us wear white T-Shirts
with *Skid's Girls* bold in black.
And when we turn around,
Skid's face's emblazoned on the back.

The music's very catchy —
you'll want to have a go.
But when Skid says, "We'll try *Duck Soup*,"
most of us groan, "Oh No!"

Amame is my favourite —
I haven't danced it yet.
But each week, if I persevere,
much better I will get.

When Skid is there in front of me,
attention I can give.
But when we face another wall,
I lose the will to live.

It's *'Coaster Step'*, or *'Sailor's Step'*,
Or, *'Shuffle Side and Rock'*;
'Two heels, two toes', *'Right fan, left fan'*,
or maybe *'Rumba Box'*.

Catherine's been there quite a while:
she's really very good.
If Skid were ever to retire
then replace him, *she* should.

Half-time, we have a cup of tea,
and, maybe, even cake.
Skid's tea is 'Milk, two sugars, stirred,'—
which should keep him awake.

Since Awel's started coming,
I think I have improved:
she shows me how to dance at home,
when she is in the mood.

In time, we'll all be perfect —
proud of us, Skid will be.
But I'm sure we'll still continue
With our lessons — wait and see!

THE BULLY

A bully is a person
who can make you very sad.
He always tries to make you feel
it's you, not him, that's bad.

A bully does not seem to need
a reason for his jibes.
He and his victims do not have
the same emotional vibes.

A bully will intimidate,
or persecute the meek,
and if you don't stand up to him
he'll think that you are weak.

A bully's never on his own:
he always has a chum.
Without this back up, I am sure,
he'd turn around and run.

A bully can and often will
make your life seem like hell.
How many kids have thought, "Thank God,"
when they hear the School bell.

Some children commit suicide
when they see no way out.
This bullying will have to stop —
of that, there is no doubt.

It isn't easy, that I know,
to rise above the taunts.

I've often thought, when I'm a ghost,
I know whom I will haunt.

A bully is a sorry sight,
and often he's the one
who's full of fear and quite a wimp,
when all is said, and done.

MEN

Why is it when men say they want
a programme on TV,
they fall asleep, and miss it all?
It seems so strange to me.

Why don't they give a realistic
time to pick you up,
instead of rushing, being late,
and finding you abrupt?

Why don't they listen when you say
you'd like a certain thing,
then swear you've never mentioned it,
and don't know what to bring?

Why don't they ever text you back
to say they are okay?
They know you always worry:
why trifle with delay?

I guess we'll never change them —
thank goodness, don't you see?
If they were always at their best,
how boring life would be!

I'M NOT A WOMEN'S LIBBER

I'm not a Women's Libber —
I can't cope without a man.
Some women might get mad at me:
consider if you can.

I like a man to open doors,
and walk on the outside

of pavements, and be there for me:
to simply be my guide.

It's nice when they pull out a chair,
before you start a meal.
I'm sure some women out there will
agree with what I feel.

Someone to carry shopping
when you've had a busy day,
and have sense of direction
when you cannot find your way.

I know we crave equality,
and that's all well and good,
but men are stronger physically:
we'd do things if we could.

I know by writing this I'm sure
some women I will vex;
but for my part, I am convinced:
we are the fairer sex.

LIFE AND DEATH

PURE CHANCE

Since I first noticed that small lump,
the thought was always there,
afraid my life would be cut short,
I thought of those who'd care.

The hospital appointment came
quite soon — too soon in fact.
The apprehension mounted then:
it left me feeling whacked.

Now, sitting in the waiting-room,
my husband at my side,
I hear the Nurse call out my name —
part of me wants to hide.

The Doctor is so very kind:
a mammogram is done.
An ultra-sound reveals a cyst:
I feel that I have won.

I'm told a cyst is nothing more
than fluid in a sac:
it can be drained, but it's so small,
I don't need to go back.

As I prepare to leave the room
a girl comes out in tears.
She obviously has had bad news:
I understand her fears.

When I come home, and carry on
with jobs that have been left,
my thoughts return reluctantly
to that young girl who wept.

I hope things work out well for her.
They have to, don't you see?
It is pure chance, that it was she,
who had bad news, not me.

LOSING A LOVED ONE

Losing a loved one is so hard to bear:
you can't get used to them not being there.
You set the table the same as before,
as you expect them to walk in the door.

You feel the need to surround yourself
with photos that show him in perfect health.
Talking is said to help many a mum
to come to terms with the damage that's done.

Family gives you the strength that you need
to get you through, with some semblance of creed.
Friends rally round; they don't know what to say
to make things right, as they were yesterday.

How will you cope with the weeks yet to come?
Never again will you want to have fun.
How dare the world carry on as before,
when you are feeling emotionally sore?

But you do know that time helps to erase
some of these feelings, but never his face.
Nothing in life, when it's all said and done,
can prepare you — for the loss of a son.

GWYNNE

The day he died, the sun it shone —
a warm September morn.
Ironically, some years before,
on this same day he was born.

He was a very private man —
not one for idle chat.
But he could be quite comical
at times — despite all that.

He was quite tall, and seemed to walk
with a lopsided gait.
His punctuality was such
that he was never late.

We've lost a very special friend —
a person we could trust;

a man who was reliable:
to him, work was a must.

The shock you feel when someone dies
so young, is hard to bear:
you can't accept that they have gone —
to you, they are still there.

I cannot seem to grasp the fact
we won't see him again.
But I know from experience,
that time *does* heal the pain.

ALZHEIMER'S

Alzheimer's is the one disease
that I have come to dread.
What causes normal people
to be ill inside their head?

It seems no matter what you eat,
or if you used to smoke.
And aluminium saucepans,
was that theory just a joke?

Respect for age it does not have,
you may be young or old,
Your dignity it takes away
and you just won't be told.

You put things in strange places,
then swear blind that you have not.
You cause such pandemonium,
but you just don't give a jot.

You lose sense of direction
so you can't find your way home.
Some gadgets are a problem,
like the simple telephone.

You get up many times each night,
you simply will not sleep.
You cannot recognise your spouse,
which gives them cause to weep.

You won't accept that you are ill:
you're sure that you are well.

You cannot see
that you are giving everybody hell.

You are convinced that you are right,
and everyone is wrong.
It must be scary, feeling
it's you — against the throng.

They say it's not inherited,
but now that Mum is ill,
my chances may well be increased,
and there's no magic pill.

If I forget, or am confused,
I think, 'Oh, here we go.'
But then I'm told, 'If you were ill,
you really would not know.'

I guess I've become paranoid
since Mum was diagnosed.
I question my behaviour —
very closely I suppose.

I do not want my children
to experience what I feel.
I think they have been through enough:
their minds would surely reel.

My husband jokes that if he goes
to make a cup of tea,
and finds soap in the teapot,
then he'll know it's conquered me.

A friend, said youngsters too forget –
it's just that they don't worry.
I guess their lives are busy,
and they're always in a hurry.

Research has shown
keeping mind active is a must:
that, with eight hours' sleep, should keep
brain free from rust.

When I'm old I'll be happy,
if Alzheimer's has not struck.
I'll hope, and pray, but really, I think —
it's down to luck.

TEGWEN

Alzheimer's is a cruel disease:
it took my Mum away;
and in her place this person,
who was 'different', shall we say.

It isn't Mum who looks at me
although it is her face:
she cannot now recall my name —
a stranger's in her place.

Hallucination plays a part:
her Mum she claims to see;
and children, though we're not sure who,
are coming home for tea.

Mum cannot seem to sleep at night:
she'll catnap in the day.
We've learnt it's wiser to agree
with what she has to say.

Her character has changed so much —
she used to be so kind.
She's now aggressive, and prone
to lash out, if she's a mind.

I cannot understand why she,
a person full of fun,
should be struck down in this harsh way:
not Tegwen — not my Mum.

It's always worse for family:
we grieve for days gone by.
Mum's happy in her own small world —
she has no need to cry.

The Mum I used to know and love
has gone, in many ways.
All I have left are memories
of carefree, childhood days.

Not only have I lost my Mum,
my Dad has lost his wife;
my children, too, have lost their Nain:
how frail the thread of life!

THE LONG GOODBYE

My Mum was in a Nursing Home
for three years, more or less,
'cause there they could look after her,
and give her what was best.

When first she went there, she would try
and open every door:
I think she was quite happy,
though of course, I can't be sure.

As time went by, she would just sit:
her words would get mixed up.
Mid-afternoon her tea would come,
in a two-handled cup.

When Carers came to move her,
she would often call my name.
For things she didn't want to do
it seems *I* got the blame.

I'd visit her, and say, "Hi, Mum!"
She, not sure what to do,
would stare at me, as if to say,
"Now, who the hell are you?"

Sometimes, she'd smile and laugh all day:
her spirits would be high —
she'd imitate the residents,
or people passing by.

On other days she'd be asleep,
or angry and dismayed.
At times like this we thought it best
that she should be obeyed.

In later months she'd be in bed
unable to get up:
she had forgotten how to eat,
and even how to suck.

I'm told this kind of illness
is now called, 'The Long Goodbye'.
From start to end it's family,
who feel the need to cry.

We would not let an animal
endure what Mum's gone through.
If only she could talk to me,
and tell me what to do.

I'm sure she'd not have wanted
to live out her days this way.
If only euthanasia
was now legal, and OK.

Towards the end, her breathing
was quite laboured, that last day.
And with her family around,
she gently slipped away.

SWITZERLAND — HERE WE COME

Whilst watching *Holby City,*
I was intrigued to see
a clinic up in Switzerland,
where you could die with ease.

Soft music would be playing,
a drink would be to hand,
your family around you:
just as you would have planned.

Thing is, it wouldn't happen,
with dementia anyway:
they'd say you couldn't make a choice —
that your judgement might be swayed.

But isn't it a pity
'cause to me it seems ideal:
a way out for the family,
and you get what you feel.

If Mum had had an option,
I think she would have gone.
She'd have seen it as a kind release —
a battle she'd have won.

So, listen all you Medics —
give people what they choose.
You'd be saving many millions:
what have you got to lose?

Though, if I get dementia,
I think I'd like to go
to Switzerland,
to end it all,
with dignity.

And so,
if I'm confused,
or muddled up,
he'll look at me,
my son,
and, with panache,
announce to all,

"Switzerland — here we come!"

TIME

INJUSTICE

Imagine you're in prison for a crime you have not done:
you took for granted all the years you went out and had fun,
You cannot understand why you've been locked up for this crime.
You're innocent, so why must it be you that's doing Time?

Your mind goes over the events that led to your arrest:
they'd learn the truth if they gave you a lie-detector test,
You're unaware that, outside, folk campaign for your release.
You long for some normality, and precious inner peace.

Your faith in British Justice has diminished overnight:
you feel so numb and tired,
that it's difficult to fight.
Your family are suffering:
they have to face the World,
which can be such a cruel place,
when angry words are hurled.

At last your case is heard in Court:
you stand there in the dock.
You see the people gathered there —
of course, some come to mock.
Eventually, you hear the words, "There's lack of evidence."
You raise your head: at last they are beginning to talk sense.

The Judge says, "You are free to go." You can't believe your ears.
You look around, but people are distorted through your tears.
Your family come up to you, and lead you through the door.
You feel the sunshine on your face, and you are free once more.

As years go by you find it very difficult to sleep:
There is a noise that haunts your dreams,
you wake up and you weep.

Acquitted you may be,
and though you're back home with the gang,
you'll take the memory to your grave,
the day the door went "Bang."

A MOTHER'S DILEMMA

Imagine that you are yourself
the mother of a man
who's killed a child, with full intent.
Consider if you can,
what would your first reaction be?
To shield, I have no doubt:
your son could not commit this crime.
The mind would shut it out.

The guilt you'd feel would be immense.
To what did you give birth?
The baby you held in your arms —
the sweetest child on earth —
has turned into a monster now,
for all the world to see.
If you could just turn back the clock
and do things differently?

You wonder where you went so wrong.
Folk look at you with scorn.
You feel your life is over now —
all you can do is mourn.
You think of your beloved son,
alone behind locked bars.
You cannot help — you might as well
be on the planet Mars.

The love you feel towards your son
is tainted now, with hate.
How dare he put you through this pain?
Reproach is far too late.
You are afraid to venture out —
scared of what people think.
Of course, all this is not your fault,
but *they* would find a link.

You think about the family
whose child's been snatched away.
While sympathy is on their side,
all you can do is pray
to God, to ask if he'll forgive
the actions of your son.
Fact is, you cannot understand,
when all is said, and done.

TIME

Time is a moment that you cannot hold:
it is more precious than silver or gold.
Time is a friend that allows you to rest,
giving you freedom to do what is best.

Time is a healer if you've been bereaved,
helping you through the first dark days of need,
until a time when you feel you can cope,
silently showing that first ray of hope.

We all complain that we can't find the time
to visit relatives: it's such a crime.
Why not act quickly, and set up a date?
Make someone happy – don't leave it too late.

Time waits for no one, it marches along
caring not whether it's right or it's wrong.
Time is the rooster that wakes you from sleep,
making quite sure that the deadline you keep.

Time seems to go so much faster these days:
I hope the rat race is only a phase.
Time will be here when we've all passed away,
quietly changing those dark nights to day.

COMING OF AGE

Coming of age can seem so exciting —
everything is so new and inviting,
Children are always impatient to be
eighteen and over, it seems sad to me.
Why can't you realize when you're well off?
Safe from outsiders, except colds and coughs,
Why all the fuss now you're able to vote?
It makes no difference, so please do not gloat,
Alcohol seems to be high on your list
but moderation, now, don't take a risk,
Parents and family want you alive:
we can but hope that you won't drink and drive.
Coming of age is not all that it seems:
responsibility — no more pipe dreams.

OUR WORLD THROUGH A PRISM

Why are we never satisfied
with things the way they are?
We grumble, moan and criticise —
like wasps stuck in a jar.

In Winter, we are all too cold:
we long for Summer sun.
But when it's here, it is too hot —
why can't we just have fun?

When it is raining, we complain,
"It's too wet to go out."
And when it's dry, we all decide
we're heading for a drought.

I think that we should look around —
they're never very far —
the ones who are less fortunate
yet, happier they are.

They see the pretty colours
that adorn this world of ours:
a rainbow that's spectacular —
a myriad of flowers.

If we could only view the world
through colours in a prism,
I'm sure we'd all be energised,
and filled with optimism.

THE INVISIBLE POWER

What makes the sky that shade of blue?
What makes the grass so green?
What makes a rainbow that curved shape?
It's perfect, have you seen?
What makes the snow a brilliant white?
What makes the rain so clear?
We take for granted all the things
that we should hold so dear.

What makes the trees so tall
that they can almost reach the sky?
Their elegance is such, you're afraid to question why.
Each snowflake is a different shape,
(or so I have been told).
Their beauty's an indulgence
that's enjoyed by young and old.
What makes a flower stand out
both in fragrance, and in hue?
What makes the birds sing out in Spring,
amidst the morning dew?
What makes the stars shine out
to give us beauty in the night?
What makes the moon change shape
and at the same time give us light?
What makes the sun give just the right
amount of warmth each day?
There must be something good out there,
to make it right, I'd say.
It's not a fluke — it can't be chance —
that's my view anyway.

THE NATIVITY

The children standing patiently
await their curtain call:
Tonight it's the Nativity
that's packed the Village Hall.

Things went quite well considering
the children are so young.
No one forgot their well-learnt lines,
or stumbled o'er their tongue.

The only mishap I recall —
the innkeeper, he said,
"Of course, you shall stay here tonight,
I've got a double-bed."

When Mary gave birth to a son,
with Joseph at her side,
three wise men came all bearing gifts,
a bright star was their guide.

The parents look so very proud,
their eyes are moist with tears.
The play has gone extremely well,
after a week of fears.

Now at the end the curtains part,
the cast stand side by side,
they bow to thunderous applause
their faces glow with pride.

They sing a merry yuletide song,
and under lights so bright,
wish us a Merry Christmas —
and a very warm goodnight.

WINTER BLUES

When clocks go back, and nights draw in,
and Winter's on its way,
I always feel a sense of loss
caused by the shorter day.

The changing weather seems to bring
us colds and coughs and flu.
I wish we had a magic pill,
with which to see us through.

Some people seem to get depressed
at this sad time of year.
Thank goodness for the Christmas fare,
to bring us joy and cheer.

The fog, the wind, the ice and snow —
all help to get us down.
If only people would smile more,
but all they do is frown.

I'm sure that lack of sunlight
is the cause of all this grief.
Our feelings take a tumble,
like a dead and falling leaf.

Then slowly, things start to improve —
cautious, without a sound:

a snowdrop finds its way
out of the hard and frozen ground.

The clocks go forward — longer days —
warm sunshine thaws the earth.
And people learn to smile again,
when Spring has given birth.

JUST A DREAM?

I've just been out — it feels like Spring.
Has Winter had its final fling?
The snow has gone — for good, I hope.
On looking back, how did we cope?

The ice was there for many weeks:
the frozen ponds too hard for beaks.
And many people lost their lives,
when dogs fell through the frozen ice.

The dogs survived: there must be here
a warning we can heed next year.
The roads were bad — there was no grip:
cars only made the vital trip.
Most people chose to stay indoors,
and got on with their household chores.

Now that the sun is out again,
the nightmare memories will wane.
When skies are blue, and grass is green,
was that hard winter just a dream?

THE LONELY TREE

Oh, lonely tree, I can but stare:
you look so cold, and dark, and bare.
Your leaves have fallen to the ground —
so quietly, without a sound.

When Winter comes, you look forlorn,
like sheep in Summer, you've been shorn:
without your cloak of velvet green
your nakedness is clearly seen.

The snow will rest on branches high.
I pray the cold won't let you die,
But you are strong: it's plain to see
you stand there, so majestically.

The world gets warmer in the spring,
and in your branches birds will sing.
They'll build their nests, and lay their eggs:
their chicks will stand on spindly legs.

Your leaves will bud, and burst anew;
you'll stand beneath a sky of blue;
you will be dressed from head to toe —
your finest greenery on show.

A MONTH SINCE CHRISTMAS

It's now a month since Christmas,
and I'm looking for a sign
to show me Spring is on its way,
and the weather will be fine.

Today I went out walking,
and much to my delight
I saw some snowdrops peeping through
the earth, to reach the light.

The days are getting longer —
the weather's not so cold.
Soon lambs will frolic in the field —
the sun will shine like gold.

The birds will sing so sweetly,
and lay their eggs in nests.
Migrating birds are back again —
our busy Summer guests.

The trees will droop with blossom;
the grass will be bright green;
these acts of nature seem to me
the best that can be seen.

Spring seems to be a busy time,
when all things grow anew.
I never cease to be amazed
at Nature's point of view.

MY POEM BOOK

I'm having a poem book published.
It's quite an exciting time:
things like this don't usually happen to me.
I'll do it whilst I'm in my prime.
I rang around quite a few people.
Mike Willmott I finally found,
he said his skill was as a proofreader,
and that he'd get things off the ground.
I sent him a few of my poems,
via e-mail, attachment of course.
He said that he'd read and amend them:
I hoped that my work he'd endorse.
He e-mailed and asked for some money,
to cover expenses to date,
so that taxman and landlord could be kept at bay —
I guess folk like that cannot wait.
A week had gone by without contact:
no e-mail from Mike did I get,
I hoped he was working on my poem book —
I think it's my nature to fret.
My son said, "He's gone with your money:
you're gullible Mum, you can't wait.
I bet he's on holiday somewhere —
you've fallen once more for the bait."
But I think my son is mistaken:
he's cynical, though kindly meant.
Mike legged it with all of my money?
No way, he's too much of a gent.

www.shrewsburybooks.com

Mary de Saulles   **41 Shropshire Recipes**   **£6.5**
The local touch: recipes for three courses from Shropshire, with origins attached.

Brenda Whincup   **Pennies in my wishing-well**   **£6.9**
Gothic poetic gems from the wry hands of Brenda, Ruyton-X1-towns poetess wi
power. Illustrated by Gerald Newton of Shrewsbury

Pauline Jones   **Makings**   **£4.9**
              More Makings   **£4.9**
Poems from Atcham, Shropshire, and Canada

Kevin Bamford   **Admiring the view**   **£4.9**
The delicious verbal delights of a meticulous observer of things beautiful. Editor f
twenty years of the Anglo-Welsh Poetry Society magazine *BORDERLINES + COMMC
SOURCE + EARTH WORKS*

Selena Trotman   **The Bath Full of Damsons**   **£9.9**
A beautiful account of an upbringing in Uffington, Uckington, and Upton Magn
Shropshire, during the 1930s.

George Richey   **Wings over Malaya**   **£8.5**
Ex-Mayor of Shrewsbury tells of exploits over the Malayan jungle, droppi
propaganda versus communism, taking part in tug-o'-war competitions in Taiping.

**Rev. Oliver Willmott Yours Reverently 1948-1953; The Parso
Knows; 1953-1968 The Vicar Calls 1968-1982 each £9.99 the set £15**
34 years' continuous commentary on Dorset life. Damian Thomson *The Dai
Telegraph* 19.09.1998 'What is amazing about them is not their quantity (750,00
words) but their amazingly consistent quality.'

Graham Dean   **A Handful of pullets**   **£6.9**
A seriously funny adult children's book about chickens

Jean McCartney   **Women who knew Jesus**   **£4.9**
'Women who got caught up with Jesus have their say'.

FORTHCOMING TITLES:

Mary de Saulles THE BOOK OF SHREWSBURY
The definitive book about Shrewsbury's history. PUBLISHER LOGASTON PRESS
LEOMINSTER

Eileen Sandford THE LITTLE PEOPLE
Ex-Mayoress of Shrewsbury, MBE's 'life full of experiences' in Nigeria, with the Gi
Guides, and as Councillor for Harlescott.

All items sent postage free UK